Animal DADS at Work

by Joanne Mattern

BeaLu
BOOKS

ISBN Hardcover: 978-1-962981-20-0
ISBN Paperback: 978-1-962981-21-7
ISBN eBook: 978-1-962981-46-0

Library of Congress Control Number: 2024950923
Publisher's Cataloging-in-Publication Data is on file with the publisher.

Edited by: Precious McKenzie
Book cover and interior design by Tara Raymo • creativelytara.com

Printed in the United States of America
November 2024
First Edition
2 7 6 5 1

BeaLu Books
Tampa, Florida

www.BeaLuBooks.com

PHOTO CREDITS: Cover: © Mircea Costina – Shutterstock, © rabuin – Shutterstock, © guentermanaus – Shutterstock; Page 4: © Natallia Ustsinava – Shutterstock; Page 5: © Mike Truchon – Shutterstock, © Ryancampbell – Shutterstock; Page 6: © Roger ARPS BPE1 CPAGB – Shutterstock; Page 7: © Mario_Hoppmann – Shutterstock; Page 8: © Swaroop Pixs – Shutterstock; Page 9: © Roger ARPS BPE1 CPAGB – Shutterstock, © Mario_Hoppmann – Shutterstock; Page 10: © Agami Photo Agency – Shutterstock; Page 11: © Wirestock Creators – Shutterstock; Page 12: © JosManuel – Adobe Stock; Page 13: © JosManuel – Adobe Stock; Page 14: © feathercollector – Shutterstock, © AndrewASkolnick – Shutterstock; Page 15: © fish1715 – Shutterstock; Page 16: © abdullatifspi – Shutterstock; Page 17: © South12th Photography – Shutterstock; Page 18: © Andrea Izzotti – Shutterstock; Page 19: © Bernard S Tjandra – Shutterstock; Page 20: © nobuhiko – Adobe Stock; Page 21: © UnknownAngel – Shutterstock; Page 22: © Toxotes Hun-Gabor Horvath – Shutterstock; Page 23: © Toxotes Hun-Gabor Horvath – Shutterstock, © Toxotes Hun-Gabor Horvath – Shutterstock; Page 24: © Bert B Wildlife Photos – Shutterstock; Page 25: © Menno Schaefer - Shutterstock; Page 26: © Robert Harding Video – Shutterstock; Page 27: © Ghost Bear – Shutterstock; Page 28: © Rafael Goes – Shutterstock Page 29: © slowmotiongli – Shutterstock; Page 30: © Uwe Bergwitz – Shutterstock; Page 31: © Andreas Wolochow – Shutterstock; Page 32: © Iuliia Timofeeva – Shutterstock; Page 33: © Le Thierry – Shutterstock; Page 34: © Dirk M. de Boer - Shutterstock; Page 35: © Uwe Bergwitz - Shutterstock

Table of Contents

INTRODUCTION

Being a parent is hard work! Moms and dads have a lot to do. They have to feed their children. They have to keep them warm. They have to protect them from **predators**. They have to make sure their babies have the best chance to grow up healthy and strong.

For most animal **species**, Mom has the full job of taking care of her young. Mama mammals, like cats, dogs, and bears, give birth without the dad even being there. They nurse their babies, keep them warm, and keep them safe. Usually, it's Mom who teaches her babies how to hunt or find food. It's a big job, and it's all on her.

Mother cat with kitten

The same is true of animals that lay eggs. For many birds, Mom sits on the eggs until they hatch. Then she feeds her babies and helps them learn to fly.

Reptiles and amphibians are a bit different. Snakes and turtles and frogs lay eggs, then leave them. These babies don't have anyone to help them when they are born. They can take care of themselves. Some reptiles, like alligators, stay close until the eggs are ready to hatch. But once the little ones pop out, Mom's job is done.

If you're thinking it's not fair that moms have to do all the work, here's some good news. There are some species where Dad helps out. Even better, some dads work really hard to take care of their young. Some even do the jobs all by themselves.

Let's meet nine animals who take male parenting to the next level. They surely belong in the Great Dad Hall of Fame!

Robin family

Baby alligator

5

Chapter One

The Lonely Dad
The Emperor Penguin

Imagine living in a place where it's cold—REALLY cold— all the time. The ground is frozen. The wind blows. It snows a lot. There's nothing but cold and ice and snow.

Now imagine raising a baby in this cold world. That's the challenge facing Daddy Emperor Penguin. His mate lays one egg. Then she goes off to find something to eat. For the next two months, Dad is home alone with the baby.

Emperor Penguin and young

Luckily, Dad has lots of tricks up his flippers to keep his egg warm. First, he puts the egg on top of his feet and tucks it under his belly. That keeps the egg from freezing on the ice. The penguin will stay that way for two months. He doesn't eat. He barely even moves. Dad knows that if the egg falls on the freezing ground, the chick inside could die.

Male Emperor Penguin

Here's some good news. Dad isn't alone. All of his buddies are doing the same. All the males get together and stand really close to each other. This keeps them warm. It also protects them from the freezing winds and storms.

Emperor Penguins keeping warm

Finally, after two months, the egg hatches. By then, Dad is pretty hungry. But he has one more job to do. Even though he hasn't eaten in months, he feeds the chick with regurgitated food from inside his throat. Then he waits for his mate to come back. When Mom shows up, it's Dad's turn to get some food. He is one dad that definitely deserves a break!

Young Emperor Penguin

Emperor Penguin feeding young

Chapter Two

The Cool Dad
The Mallee Fowl

Mallee Fowl live in Australia. These birds are about the size of a large chicken. They live on the ground and build their nests on the ground as well. Building and taking care of that nest is Dad's number-one job.

A male Mallee Fowl can take up to a year to build a nest. He uses his long legs to dig in the soft earth. He gathers leaves and dirt into a big mound. Finally, the nest is ready.

The female Mallee bird starts laying her eggs. She will lay an egg every four to eight days, until there are about 24 eggs in the nest. The eggs are laid in a hole at the top of the mound. Dad then covers them with leaf **litter**. Then his job really starts.

Mallee Fowl standing on nest

The eggs have to be kept at the same temperature if they are going to hatch. Since nests don't have **thermostats**, it's up to Dad to keep things cool. He takes this job very seriously.

The male is always checking the temperature. If it's cold, he adds more dirt and leaves. If it's hot, he takes some dirt and leaves off. That's a big job! The female helps out a bit, but it's mostly Dad who does all the work.

After 60 days, the eggs start hatching. And here's the funny part. After all that work keeping the nest just right, the Mallee Fowl parents don't take care of their babies at all! As soon as the chicks hatch, they have to take care of themselves.

Young Mallee Fowl

Chapter Three

The Quiet Dad
Darwin's Frog

These frogs live in Chile and Argentina in South America. They're named after a British scientist, Charles Darwin. He was the first European to discover and describe these frogs.

Darwin's Frogs are really small—only about an inch and a half long. But the dads have a big job. The male stands by while the female lays about 40 eggs into the leaves on the forest floor. The male **fertilizes** the eggs, but that's just the beginning of his role.

Daddy frog stays close by for about three weeks until the frog **larvae** start moving inside the eggs. Then he swallows the eggs! But don't worry, he hasn't eaten his babies. Instead, the eggs stay safe inside a vocal **sac** in his throat. Frogs usually make noise with this sac. But since the Darwin's Frog's sac is full of eggs, he can't make any noise at all. He can't eat either.

Darwin's Frog

About three days later, the larvae hatch into tiny tadpoles. Still, Dad keeps them in his vocal sac. They stay there for another 50 to 70 days. The father frog feeds them with liquid inside the sac and with the yolk from the eggs.

Finally, it's time for the baby frogs to move out. They wiggle into their father's mouth. Dad finds a stream, then spits the eggs into the water. From then on, the little frogs are on their own. Dad can get something to eat and make some noise!

Darwin's Frog

Chapter Four

The Sticky Dad
The Giant Water Bug

Giant Water Bugs live all over North America. This bug is a real tough character, attacking other insects and even frogs and small birds. A Water Bug's bite is very painful. Even worse, it injects digestive juices that quickly make a meal out of its **prey**.

Giant Water Bug

Giant Water Bug enjoying a meal

A Water Bug is tough, but when it comes to taking care of his babies, Dad is a real softie...uh, we mean real sticky.

A Giant Water Bug female can lay up to 150 eggs at a time. She lays the eggs right on the male's back and glues them there with a sticky goo. Now it's Dad's job to care for the eggs. For the next week or two, he swims with all those eggs stuck to his back. It's a very odd thing to see, but it's the best way to keep the eggs safe.

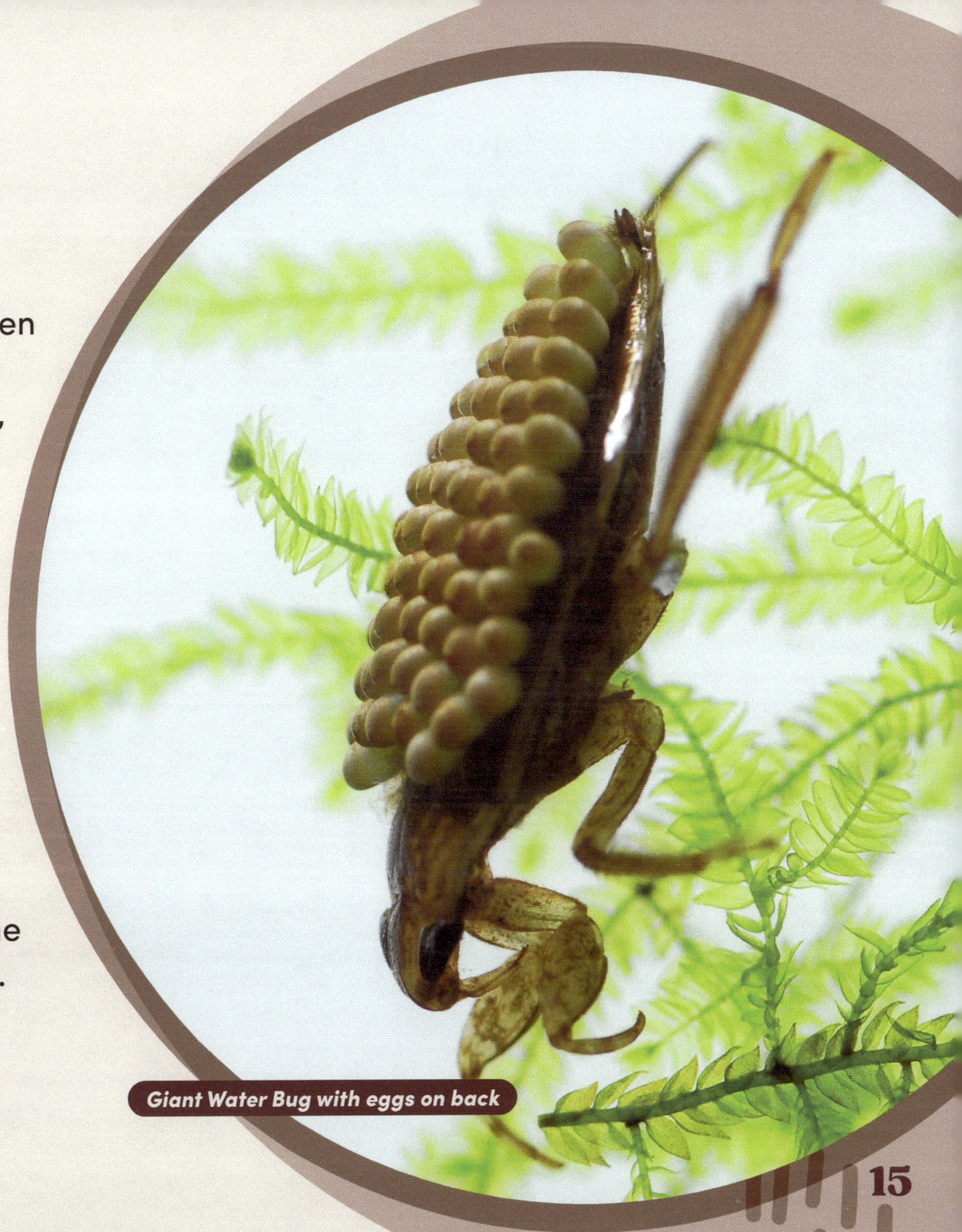

Giant Water Bug with eggs on back

Even better, Dad makes sure the eggs get enough air to survive. Sometimes the bug does this by swimming to the surface. Other times, Dad does what looks like push-ups under the water. This swirls fresh water around the eggs and brings air bubbles to the babies growing inside.

Giant Water Bug pushing eggs to surface

Finally, the eggs hatch. The babies, which are called nymphs, can take care of themselves right away. They swim away from Dad without even saying thank you.

Giant Water Bug Nymph

Chapter Five

The Pregnant Dad
The Seahorse

So far we've seen some dads that take care of their babies by staying close and keeping them safe and warm. But these fathers don't actually carry their babies in their bodies. However, there is one animal that does just that! Meet Mr. Mom, also known as the seahorse.

Seahorses are actually fish. They get their name because their face is shaped just like a little horse. Unlike other fish, seahorses have a very special way to give birth

Male Seahorse

The male and female seahorses spend some quality time together. They swim with their tails linked together. Then, the female performs a special dance for the male. Scientists think this helps the male's body get ready to carry the eggs. A female seahorse lays her eggs—right into the male's body!

The female can lay up to 2,000 eggs at a time inside the male. The eggs hatch inside a special sac on the male's belly called a brood pouch. The dad even looks **pregnant**, because his belly puffs up as the babies get bigger.

Seahorses swimming together

About 45 days later, the pouch opens. The father's body pushes and squeezes the babies out. The babies, called fry, shoot out into the water. What a super dad!

Male Seahorse and babies

But wait! Dad doesn't take care of his babies after they are born. The little ones are on their own. And here's a shock: If the babies are still around when the dad is ready to eat, sometimes he will snack on his own babies! Okay, he's really hungry, but that is not a good way for a dad to act!

Why do male seahorses carry their babies? Scientists think this allows the female to lay more eggs instead of having to wait until her babies are born. This helps keep the species alive and helps a unique sea creature survive.

Young Seahorses

Chapter Six

The Tough Dad
The Stickleback

Lots of moms and dads protect their kids. This is true of animals too. Even fish can be pretty tough when it comes to keeping their babies safe. And no fish is tougher than the Stickleback. This fish dad makes protection his number one job.

Male Sticklebacks produce a sticky glue and use it to make a nest. After a female comes along and lays her eggs there, the male fish chases her away. From now on, all he cares about is taking care of those eggs.

Dad has two big problems to worry about. One is making sure the eggs receive enough air. He uses the little fins on the sides of his body to fan the eggs. This moves fresh water around the nest and washes away any waste material. A Stickleback fans its fins up to 400 times a minute. And he can keep up this workout for hours.

Adult Stickleback

The second problem is keeping the babies safe from predators. To do this, Dad stays near the nest. Any animal that comes along for a snack gets chased away. A Stickleback might only be about seven inches long (18 cm), but he doesn't let his size stop him!

Once the eggs hatch, Dad's job gets harder. Now he has to make sure his little babies, or fry, don't swim into trouble. If a predator comes too close, Dad has a good trick up his fins. He gulps down the babies and hides them in his mouth. Dad will also do this if his children swim too far from the nest. Once Dad has grabbed his small fry, he spits them back into the nest. Then he gets back to guard duty.

Stickleback with eggs

Stickleback and fry

23

Chapter Seven

The Paws-On Dad
The Red Fox

Some mammal dads aren't very paws-on. After they mate with the female, the male often goes his own way. Red foxes are different. These dads are real family guys.

Red Fox and young

Male and female foxes stay together for life. The female gives birth to two to seven babies, called kits, in a den. Both parents take care of the babies. While the mother stays in the den and nurses her kits, Dad goes out to find food. Mice, gophers, and birds are this animal's favorite things to eat. Fruit and nuts taste good too. Daddy Fox makes sure to bring plenty of treats home to his little family.

Red Fox with meal

When the kits are about three months old, it's time for them to come out of the den. To get them to go outside, Dad stops bringing them food. Instead, he hides prey around the outside of the den. This helps the kits learn to find food and hunt for themselves. That's just one of the lessons Dad and Mom teach their babies.

Red Fox kit

Fox dads also like to play. They wrestle and tumble with their little ones. Sometimes they chase the young foxes. This helps the babies learn to stay safe from predators. Older brothers and sisters also help out. Being part of a fox family sounds like fun!

Male Red Fox playing with kits

Chapter Eight

The Single Dad
The Rhea

Rheas are tall birds that cannot fly. They live in South America. Rhea dads take parenting very seriously. In fact, they do all the parenting by themselves.

Rhea and young

One male Rhea lives with up to 10 or 12 females. He mates with all of them. Once the females lay their eggs, their job is done. The male Rhea doesn't want any help from Mom. In fact, he will chase all the females away from the nest. For the next 40 days, Dad sits on the nests. He keeps the eggs warm and safe.

Male Rhea nesting eggs

Rhea rounding up young

Once they hatch, Dad still has lots of work to do. Now he has 50 or more children to take care of, all by himself. Dad brings the young birds food. He keeps them safe by letting them shelter under his wings. He chases away predators. And since these birds are about five feet tall (1.5 meters) and weigh up to 88 pounds (39 kilograms), most predators get the message and get lost.

Sometimes a male Rhea will even adopt a chick that has lost its parents. Dad keeps up the hard work for at least two years.

Rhea are related to two other flightless birds. Those birds are the ostrich and the emu. Male ostriches and emus also take care of their babies. It just goes to show that being unable to fly doesn't mean a bird can't be a great dad.

Rhea and older chick

Chapter Nine

The Responsible Dad
The Marmoset

Mama Marmosets have it rough. These little monkeys only weigh about eight ounces (224 grams) and are just seven inches (18 cm) long. Females almost always give birth to twins. Those twins weigh about two ounces (56 grams). They can be up to 25 percent of the mother's body weight. That would be like a 120-pound (54 kilograms) human giving birth to two 15-pound (7 kilograms) babies!

Marmoset family

It's no surprise that Mom needs some help after giving birth to two big babies. Luckily, Dad is right there to help. Right after the mother gives birth, Dad licks the babies to clean them. Then he puts the babies on his back, where they hang on for dear life. For the next two weeks, Dad brings the babies to their mother when they need to nurse. Otherwise, the babies ride piggyback 24/7.

Marmoset carrying baby

After two or three months, the babies are ready for solid food. Once again, Dad takes charge. He finds fruit and mashes it up, then feeds it to his little babies. Marmosets also like to eat sweet sap and nectar.

Marmoset preparing food for young

A Marmoset family stays together. Males and females mate for life. Their adult children sometimes stay with the family all their lives. These animal dads help make sure their family stays safe and healthy.

The animals in this book are very different from each other. But they all have one big thing in common. Whether they are carrying their babies, protecting their nests, or teaching their young ones how to survive, these creatures are the best dads in the animal world!

Marmoset family

GLOSSARY

fertilizes—to make an egg able to produce a baby

larvae—insects that have hatched out of an egg

litter—small bits of leaves found on the ground

predators—animals that hunt other animals for food

pregnant—carrying a baby inside its body

prey—animals that are eaten by other animals

sac—a small pouch

species—a group of animals that are the same

thermostats—a device that senses changes in temperature

ABOUT THE AUTHOR

Joanne Mattern has written more than 350 books for children. Many of her books focus on science, social studies, history, and biography, and her publishers include Running Press, Enslow, Lerner, and Scholastic.

www.ingramcontent.com/pod-product-compliance
Lightning Source LLC
Chambersburg PA
CBHW041552030426

42335CB00005B/192